MW00785928

The Life and Times of Blind Boy Billy

Y'all Don't Know the Half of It

Bill Wharton
(The Sauce Boss)

ISBN 978-0-692-17309-1

To listen to the songs while reading this book,
go to sauceboss.com/bbbsoundtrack

Front cover photo by Ruth Wharton
Back cover photo by Eric Ilasenko

Killer Tone
I got busted knuckles, I got broken bones
I got wore out muscles, I got trouble at home
I got bad credit, got an overdrawn loan
But I don't care, 'cause I got killer tone

Got myself busted, and I got myself robbed
Wrecked my El Camino, and I lost my job
No employment, my money's all blown
But I don't care, 'cause I got killer tone

This ain't no fable, my story is true
It happened to me, it could happen to you
I done lost most everything I own
But I don't care, 'cause I got killer tone

When I got to the top of the mountain, something clicked. Halfway up the mountain, Bob said, "If I get lost in these mountains, I always go for the highest peak." But when I got to the top of the mountain, after being pushed, and dragged, and cajoled ("come on you can do it"), and me struggling to get that last 100 yards that was, I swear, at least a mile. The day after being released from the Tucson Medical Center with a temperature of 105 degrees, and strict orders from the doctor to go to bed and not get up for three days. The day I ate six peyote buttons, climbed thousands of feet, sweating and spewing from every orifice all over that mountain, and ralphing my guts out; after all that, Bob turned to me and said, "I'm the guy that guys like you write about."

After all that, I figured I was just gonna have to go out and do some stuff rather than sit around and write little diddleys. And do stuff, I did. And when I got to the bottom of that mountain...I was well.

This is the backstory behind the music. It's been an adventure. I did not get that killer tone by sitting around writing little diddleys. Killer tone happened to me.

The brakes fail in my truck on a one-lane bridge, with a truck full of rednecks traveling at five miles an hour in front of me. Either rear-end the truck, or go over the side with my whole damn family. Luckily, the truck in front of me was one of those big-tire, high-off-the-ground, mud-boggin' vehicles, so no bumpers were involved. The body of my freshly painted 1959 El Camino "gently" wrapped around the motor, cushioning the blow, and miraculously, no one was hurt. The time I was busted twice within a month for crimes related to the possession of cannabis (almost three times). All the broken bones I suffered as a kid. The time I was fired from Sloppy Joe's in Key West. The trouble I had staying solvent while stubbornly playing my own music, and the trouble I gave my wife over the last half century. The countless incidents with pickpockets, neighbors, band mates, plagiarists, sharks, crackheads, junkies, and child molesters, all taking something from me that I will never get back. All true. So here I am, about to show my ass, dumb as it may be. And like a lot of memoirs, most of what follows is also true. But one truth is undeniable. I do have KILLER tone.

10

My first memory is one of song. My mama pushing me in the swing in the park by the lake, in that Florida salmon-rose twilight.

Jesus loves me, this I know.
For the Bible tells me so.
 "Higher"
 Sung with a gentle detachment from the realities around her, she was in that space. The now of everything.
Little ones to him belong.
They are weak but he is strong.
 "Higher"
Yes, Jesus loves me.
Yes, Jesus loves me.
Yes, Jesus loves me.
The Bible tells me so.
 "HIGHER"

I was a mama's boy. My mama loved me, and I loved her more than anything. But that was not the half of it. She sang for redemption. She sang in that space that discounts nothing. That space that has no accentuation. No exclamation. A simple song with her own ultimate reality. And me, a toddler, oblivious to the rape of the orphaned young woman, and subsequent abortion, just wanted to go higher. She gave me that space, and I carry it with me always.

This opus is dedicated to my Mama.
Viola Crittenden Wharton

When people ask me, "Where'd ya learn to cook?" I always say: "My Mama!" She won a Betty Crocker cooking contest with her Salmon Haystacks recipe. She showed me how to cook from scratch. With love.

Salmon Haystacks

Preheat oven to 350 degrees
16 oz can of salmon
1 egg
2 Tbsp catsup
2 Tbsp mayonnaise
4 Tbsp Liquid Summer Hot Sauce (my embellishment)
½ cup chopped onions
1 cup bread crumbs
Mix and make little "haystacks."
Bake for 20 minutes.

Mama was a gooood cook, in the southern tradition. She would take a dollar and make a dinner for a family of seven, while carrying a heavy weight throughout... until she was finally diagnosed with schizophrenia. In the hospital, the convulsions produced by the electroshock "therapy" broke her back. Her recovery was long and hard, and for the rest of her life she would occasionally slip back into that place where time creeps by, and the weight would return.

She would find solace in cooking and caring for her family. Once I got the call: "Mama's freakin' out. She's cookin' pies." She missed her kids, so she began cooking pies. She didn't say anything, she just started cooking pies...lots of pies. "She's goin' crazy with pies!" Blackberry pies, peach pies, her specialty: lemon icebox pie, pecan pies, rhubarb pies, all kind of pies. When she finished her 27th pie, her entire family was sitting at the table.

We would come to visit, and she would make her doughnuts for breakfast. Not just doughnuts, no. Y'all don't know the half of it. Not just doughnuts. Not just glazed doughnuts. Not just buttermilk doughnuts, no. Glazed buttermilk POTATO doughnuts! Hot out of the pan. And the first thing out of her mouth after breakfast was, "What do y'all want for lunch?" That's where I got it from.

Glazed Buttermilk Potato Doughnuts

2 eggs
1 cup sugar
1 cup cold mashed potatoes
1 cup buttermilk
1 tsp salt
4 cups flour
1 Tbsp baking powder
1 tsp baking soda
1 tsp nutmeg
Glaze: Mix 1 cup confectioners' sugar with ½ cup milk.
Sift dry ingredients. Add the rest of the ingredients
Chill overnight. Heat 3 cups of oil until it shimmers.
Drop a tablespoon of dough into the oil, a few at a
time. Remove and drop each donut into the glaze.
Enjoy while still hot.

Mama's Cookin' (For Viola)

Mama's in the kitchen, baking her bread
Everybody gonna get fed
She's on a mission, checking the beans
Cookin' on top of the stove
Mama's in the kitchen, get out of the way
Ain't no place to play
We all gonna have some o' Mama's cookin' today

Mama's in the kitchen, choppin' it up
Just need one more cup
She's on a mission, look at her go
Running to and fro
Mama's in the kitchen, stuffing the bird
I'll be back for thirds
Ain't nobody can beat my Mama's cookin'

Squash casserole and pole beans
Angel biscuits
Fried chicken and collard greens
Blackberry surprise
Turkey gravy and giblets
Salmon haystacks
Buttermilk potato doughnuts
First thing in the morning
Lemon icebox pie

Mama's in the kitchen, stirrin' the pot
See what the pantry got
She's on a mission, takin her time
At 300 degrees
Mama's in the kitchen, is it ready?
Will be by and by
I can't wait for Mama's rhubarb pie

I came up around Orlando, Florida, next to a swamp. I loved the wild. Still do. I hung out with raccoons, fox squirrels, moccasins, rattlesnakes, and alligators. My first encounter with a gator was when I was very young. Two boys who lived next door brought a gator they caught in the lake behind our house. I was just tall enough to peer into the trunk of their car. They had bound the gator's mouth and legs, but they paid for it. They were cut up pretty good, where the gator had sliced them with tail and claws. Go back to that lake today and there are no alligators. The sprawl of Disney has consumed them. The mouse ate the gators. It's difficult to live with Jurassic Park in your backyard. Hard on the Schnauzer. Some places in Florida, they're thriving. There's a slaughterhouse down in Central Florida on a lake. It's pretty creepy after the sun goes down. So, this murky tale is about the hunt in the swirling currents caused by something swimming in the dark waters down underneath.

The group on the recording of *Alligator* is a trio. I did my one-man band setup with Lucky Peterson playing bass and Pat Ramsey playing harp.

Alligator

Alligator
On the sunny side
Alligator
I'm gonna get your hide
Alligator
Like a pair of shoes
Alligator
He got the 12-gauge blues
Alligator
I'm gonna get my wish
Alligator
You're my favorite dish

Marinated Pork Tenderloin Stuffed with Garlic

1 pork tenderloin butterflied
3 heads garlic peeled
Stuff the loin with the garlic and tie it together.
Marinate for a few days.
Baste with the marinade as you grill.

Liquid Summer Orange Juice Marinade
1 small can orange juice concentrate, thawed
2 oz of Liquid Summer Datil Pepper Hot Sauce
2 Tbsp honey
2 Tbsp mustard
This marinade is great for pork, chicken, fish, rattlesnake, or alligator. For steak, substitute red wine for the orange juice. It also doubles as a dipping sauce.

Writing all this down has been great therapy for me. I feel like I can tell you, the reader, things I've never told anyone before.
Like the time...
Well...

When I was a boy passing into juvenescence, I lived at the end of a long dirt road, with sand so deep it would scald your ankles. Behind the house was a swamp, and there was a secluded little logging trail cut through the woods, where we would stage our make-believe battles, and run and play. I was growing fast and searching for my self. Where do I begin and where do I end? Who/what/how am I? I loved being in the woods. I felt like I was part of it, along with all the creatures and the trees.

I was walking down this path all by myself. I had this impulse to take off my clothes. I took off my shoes and shirt, dropped my pants and walked through the forest. It was totally liberating. I felt like all the squirrels, and 'coons, and snakes were cheering me on my victory lap. "You go little fella. You just like us. We don't need no stinkin' pants!!! We don't need no school! We don't need no people tellin' us what to do. We know what to do! We in the woods!"

And then... I fell in love. It was not puppy love. Here is my confession.

I had a relationship with a tree. I know that sounds strange and kinky, but it's not what you think. A few miles from my house was a tree. I would sometimes walk to where that tree lived and hang out with that tree. I would stand in front of that tree... and I would be with that tree. It felt like that tree knew I was there. We were together. This was not just any tree. This was a 3,500-year-old cypress, estimated to be the fifth oldest tree in the world. At 3,500 years old, you probably know what's going on. Before the hurricane of 1925, it was 165 feet tall, stretching far above the canopy in regal radiance. This was "The Big Tree." It had a diameter of 17 ½ feet. *Had* a diameter of 17 ½ feet. On January 16, 2012, it was destroyed by an arsonist. I cried like a baby.

He was 12 when his father bought a $15 Silvertone guitar from Sears, and they shared it. About that same time, playing drums in the marching band at school, he would beat on any and everything. Whatever was in front of him. Pots and pans out of the cupboard, spread out on the kitchen floor, the top of his desk at school, the dinner table, anything. Marking time at his desk, a nervous child composing rapid fire 16th note marching cadences only he could hear in a virtual parade by grinding his teeth back and forth as the teacher droned on through the boring afternoon. Soon, it would be after-school band practice. He was learning the mechanics after school, and practicing during English, Math, and History. Also, a mischievous child, he drove his teachers crazy with dynamics. Jamming on the resonant steel desk out of sight between his legs very softly at ppp (triple piano, or very, very soft) and slowly crescendo to f (forte or loud). It was ppp for a minute, then pp for a few minutes, working up to p for a while, then pf, on to mf (moderate forte) just below the teacher's threshold of hearing. Then he would decrescendo, backing down to ppp and start the process again and again, each time getting a little bit louder until the climax when her head would explode as she realized what had been happening for the last 15 minutes. He was happiest when making an awful racket.

Photo: John Peterson

At 15, I worked all summer in the snack bar at
Sanlando Springs, serving up hot dogs, candy bars,
and sodas. I saved every penny. In the fall I took my
earnings and bought a drum set. I was in business.

My first gig was at Simonelli's Italian Restaurant. The quintet split $35 and a pizza. We were hooked. At 17 I landed a gig playing at the Club Juana in Orlando. I was actually too young to be in the place, so David Miller, the bandleader, said, "When the suits come in the front door, you go out the back 'til they are gone." It was 1965. I was fresh outta high school, and this cover band played the coolest top 40 there ever was. The New Englanders played six nights a week, nine-to-two, 45 on and 15 off. In addition to the British Invasion stuff, we did all the R&B hits: James Brown, Wilson Pickett, Jr. Walker, Sam and Dave, Ray Charles, Righteous Brothers, Otis Redding. And folk-rock stuff that was big at the time: The Byrds, Dylan, We Five, The Seekers. We were killing the Zombie tunes. Also, we did the blues of Jimmy Reed, Muddy Waters, Chuck Berry, Slim Harpo, Mose Allison, and Paul Butterfield, to name a few. Dave Miller was a walking jukebox. He took me under his wing and taught me how to really play, and how to do a show. He could do anything on a guitar. He could hold any audience, large or small. There's a part of him in every one of my performances. After being on the gig a couple of months, I made that mistake that I always made, and he kicked me in the butt, right in front of everybody. I learned to play the guitar by avoiding his foot. We did choreography, tight four-part harmony, and we had matching attire. Occasionally, I would forget what day of the week it was, and show up in the wrong clothes. Some folks thought I was the leader of the band since I was dressed differently. But no, I was forgetful, going to college by day and rockin' and rollin' at night. My "education" was raging in every direction. I had a blast.

David Miller, BW, Mike Notartomaso, Nick Holmes

On Sunday we'd hit the Vanguard in Cocoa Beach, alternating sets with national touring acts. I soaked it all up. Wayne Cochran and the C. C. Riders were regulars there. They would come through Brevard County every couple of months for a stop on the beach. The Showmen were also regulars. They would later change their name to The Vanilla Fudge. It was a happening scene. Cocoa Beach was a little beach town with a high IQ, thanks to the influx of astronauts, aerospace engineers and scientists at the Cape. Brevard also had the best surfing on the East Coast. There was some great cross pollination of the musician, surf, nerd, biker, hot rod, and underground cultures at the Vanguard. Murph the Surf, the famous diamond thief, would hang out there. I relished the excitement and intrigue.

During my first year of college, I stayed in Orlando with Mimi, my grandmother. Mary Hill Wharton was a gentile lady from South Carolina, who taught me how to cheat at solitaire. She wasn't the best cook, but she had a dish that was dynamite. She would stuff oranges with sweet potatoes for Christmas dinner.

Mimi's Sweet Potatoes

3 large sweet potatoes
6 oranges
Dash of each: cinnamon, allspice, cloves
3 Tbsp maple syrup
Bake the potatoes. Cut the oranges in half, and juice them. Cut off a little slice off of the bottoms of the orange halves so they stay flat on the cookie sheet without rolling over. Mix ½ cup of the juice with the other ingredients, and fill the orange cups. Put a marshmallow on top of each cup, and bake at 350 degrees for 15 or 20 minutes.

In 1966, Ruthie, my high school sweetheart, and I got jobs at a summer camp in North Carolina. We were counselors, each in charge of cabins full of kids. I was the camp's official folk singer, leading the singing after supper. We taught Nature Study during the day, and studied nature at night. Y'all don't know the half of it. Let's just say it sealed the deal. A few months later we were married. And then we started a family.
And it wasn't long before there were four of us.

Somehow, we scraped by. It didn't cost so much to live back then. When Annie and Mary were around three and four, we had a Christmas that was really tight. Ruth was in tears because we only had $15 to buy gifts for the girls. We went to a toy store specializing in model trains and little toy soldiers and such. We bought a few little farm animals. A cow and a horse, three chickens, and a duck. We bought an eagle. The biggest investment was a hippopotamus that we got for a dollar and a half.

On Christmas eve, after the girls were asleep, I went out in the backyard and found a sheet of plywood. I grabbed some rocks, and some moss. I put together a little diorama, painting the wood and making a mountain from the rocks, and trees from the moss. Lights shone down on the tiny pasture with livestock and the eagle perched on the hill. The hippo reigned supreme. Twenty years later the girls told us, "That was the best Christmas we ever had."

28

Cadillac of a Woman

When all of the angels up in heaven
Came down to find a bride
You know they heard the same old story
All over the countryside
So, they climbed up their ladder
And then they flew to their beds
That's where they told their story
These are the words that they said

She's a diamond deluxe
She's a Cadillac of a woman

So, it's away in a manger
Got no crib for a bed
Try to keep out of danger
And try to keep that little fella fed
Mary, she loved little Jesus
She loved him the best that she could
And you know that's why little Jesus
Turned out to be solid good

She was a diamond deluxe
She was a Cadillac of a woman

Photo: Jon Nalon

When I moved to Tallahassee, there was not much of a music scene, so I started writing my own songs, doing what local gigs I could find, and just jamming for the sake of jamming. We were able to stray from typical forms and genres, mashing up jazz, classical, folk, blues, rock, or whatever into a kaleidoscopic experience that was very loose and freeform. Not only was the music experimental, so was our intake of psychedelics. The combination was a potent brew of creative energy. It helped us to understand what it means to be deep inside the music. Once we had a nonstop, 11-hour jam session. Many of us were cutting our cosmic teeth at this time, searching the far reaches of what was possible. It was an awesome time to be coming of age.

Ray Brooks, Jim Farr, Waldo Hunter, BW
Photo: Colman Rutkin

The idea for the funky ragtime jump tune, *Blind Boy Billy* was originally a drawing. Right after coming down from an otherworldly adventure on psilocybin, I wrote *Cadillac of a Woman*, and a few other tunes. Also, I doodled some abstract meanderings along with a few words that would become *Blind Boy Billy*. Somehow it all morphed into a tune about a notorious character and musician, whose only plan was to play all the time.

Blind Boy Billy

Blind Boy Billy he's the fat man with the razor
He's the keeper of the keys
Blind Boy Billy he's the fat man with the razor
He's the keeper of the keys

All up and down on the Eastern Seaboard
Blind Boy Billy called his home
With a hundred miles of gasoline,
Five hundred miles to go
And a thousand miles of mamas all alone

Blind Boy Billy used to sing this song
Play that fiddle all night long
Play the saxophone, play that drum
Play so loud that the police come
Blind Boy Billy's shovin' em in
Hittin' his face and hittin his chin
He don't care what the police say
Gonna play that fiddle to the break of day

Blind Boy Billy, it's all the same
He don't need to plan the game
Nickel on the table, dime in the pocket
Finger on the trigger
And an eye in the socket

Once upon a time, the goose drank wine
The monkey spit tobacco on the streetcar line
Streetcar broke, the monkey choked
And they all had to go to town on a billy goat
But that old Billy kept on walkin'
He just kept on talkin', awww yeah
Gonna play that fiddle to the break of day
Play that fiddle, play that fiddle
Play that fiddle to the break of day
Blind Boy Billy gonna play the blues away

Album art: Dick Bangham

Then there was the Wild Blue Yonders. The original lineup had trumpet, flute, violin, and a soprano who sang mostly an ethereal scat over the top of everything. I was the singer/songwriter/acoustic guitar player. No drummer, no bass player. The violinist, David Davidson, would leave Tallahassee to become the concertmaster of the Jacksonville symphony, then to Nashville where he became the go-to violinist in town.

Art design: Dick Bangham

Almost 45 years after the Wild Blue Yonders played, David produced my *Blind Boy Billy* album, so here we are. You can hear him ripping the solo in the title cut, and ripping your heart out with his viola in *Lonely Girl*, and pulling out all the stops with his exquisite string arrangement on *Pleasures of the Deep*.

Pleasures of the Deep

All out on the highway
All out on the sea
All out on the skyway
There's a song that wants to be

That's when you came up to me
You came to see right through me
You came and you knew me
You came and you blew me away

Chorus
You got me walking in my sleep
You brought me precious stones to keep
You got me undivided; you got me undivided
You got me undivided with your pleasures of the deep.

You never had to sell me
You never had to tell me
You never had to do a thing
You just lay right down in my song

That's when you came to know me
That's when you came to show me
Underneath of the sky
Ain't no how, ain't no why

One morning in the '70s, I walked out in my front yard, and leaning up against my daughter's bicycle was a National Steel Guitar. I saw it there, and I looked around. There was nobody. Then I took a good look at it and realized how old it was. A Hawaiian scene with volcanos and palm trees and the moon and stars and a little man in a boat is etched on the back. Whoa! Turns out it was made in 1933. Was this the guitar from God? Did the devil put it there so I could play his blues? What the fuck's going on around here? It was not long before the National began speaking to me. You ask any real guitar player, and they will tell you a guitar has its own voice, and if you listen, you will hear what it has to say. That guitar spoke to me. It led me down a deep blues path. Late at night, after the traffic died, and the bustle of town settled, and nobody was stirring, I could hear it. I would put a slide on those strings, and that guitar would sing! And I would listen.

I listened to that guitar for a decade or more. Then one day, Herb Williams dropped by the house. Herb was a conceptual artist, a pilot, and an adventurer. He fabricated screen windows for his old Chevrolet for travel in bug-ridden areas. He had traveled to South America to get in on the gold rush. After a long conversation, he slyly asked, "Did you ever figure out who left that guitar in your yard?" He was leaving town and had to lighten his load. "I bet Bill could use this." I had long since resigned myself to the fact that the National was a loaner. When I leave this world, I'll lend it to someone else to play for a while. For now, it hangs on my wall within easy reach.

1933 National Style O

Your Maytag Done Broke Down

Baby Doll, Baby Doll
You know your Maytag done broke down
It's been too long since your
Handyman come around

Baby Doll, Baby Doll
Don't believe everything on TV
You know them commercials
Put out by the Maytag Company

You need some service
I mean right away
Cause if you don't
Your dirty clothes gonna stay that way

I'm gonna check your motor
Make sure your belt is tight
I 'm 'onna grease it good
Make that thing run just right
Baby Doll, Baby Doll
You know your Maytag done broke down
Been too long since your
Handyman come around

BBQ Hash

Keep cookin' it down until most of the liquid has cooked away.

I was named after my grandfather, William Watts Wharton Senior. We called him Pop. He was my first character role model. When I slip into the Sauce Boss persona and dialect, I'm channeling his way of talking. He would joke and tell foxhole stories from the first World War. He would take out his false teeth and scare the hell out of us little kids. Many stories in our family were told sitting around eating his South Carolina BBQ hash. A few departures from his recipe: I sometimes smoke the meat first, and also, I use my Liquid Summer Hot Sauce.

My Granddaddy's BBQ Hash

2 lb beef chuck roast
3 lb pork boneless Boston butt
½ cup apple cider vinegar
2 bottles of Heinz Chili Sauce
¼ cup honey
Liquid Summer Hot Sauce to taste

Trim excess fat from meat. Cut it up in one-inch cubes, and cover with water in a large cast iron pot. Boil the meat until tender. Take the meat out of the broth and shred it, discarding any bones or fat. Put the meat back into the broth. Add vinegar, chili sauce, and honey. Cook it down until the juice is almost all gone. Add the Liquid Summer Hot Sauce. Serve on a bun with a big slice of onion and a splash of Liquid Summer.

I wrote *Let the Big Dog Eat*, and some things started to come together for me. Filmmaker Jonathan Demme (*The Silence of the Lambs, Philadelphia, Stop Making Sense, Married to the Mob*) heard the tune and put it in his movie, *Something Wild*. A few bands were covering the tune as well as *Blind Boy Billy* and *Cadillac of a Woman*. I was feeling pretty sporty, but I had a hankering to do something larger. I had some traveling to do.

Let the Big Dog Eat

Way down South, in the rain and the heat
Sure gets hot down there, you could
Cook an egg on the concrete
Everybody on the city street says
Whoa! Let the big dog eat

Call the doctor, call the nurse
Don't know what it is
But I know it sure hurts
Call the ambulance, call the cops
Call the number of the man of God
Let the big dog eat

Photo: A guy named Ed

Back in those days I was ready to go. I did some traveling here and there. There was a drummer who played with me for a while, who was hanging out in Tucson, and having a pretty good time of it. He said, "Come on out. We'll jam." So, I grabbed my old National Steel Guitar and stuck out my thumb. I had a beautiful trip out, being free, with no schedule, no hassles, just the road and the rides, and the characters who picked me up. By the time I got to Tucson, my buddy had copped a gig, and hightailed it to California. So, I'm walkin' down 4th Avenue, all "what now," and stepped into some kind of adventure movie. That's when I met Don Peyote, and Frog, and Bob. And Señor Mescalito. Frog comes up and strikes up a conversation, then Bob and Don Peyote join us and the first thing I know, I'm right in the middle of an Arizona smuggling ring, having beers and doing business. Cool!

Bob asks me, "What's up?" And I tell them the story, and he invites me over to the house for a few days. Way cool! It was a great time just going with the flow, enjoying Tucson and getting a view of the "culture." I checked out the mountains. I happened upon a little street fair and wandered into a little makeshift stand, the guy selling beads and talismans and charms. A little tin bell caught my eye. Don't know why I bought it. A little rusty thing that went, "Ching, ching." When I picked it up he said to me, "Good luck." As I tied the bell to the handle of my guitar case, I was thinking, "Maybe this will help keep us together." After a few days I was ready to move on, so Bob says, "Why don't you take something home with you. It's winter and the mota bueno is happening."

I bought a brick of Mexican weed for 80 bucks. I also got a pound of unpressed Michoacán buds for $100. It looked like a bag of peacock feathers. It was beautiful! I was traveling very light, just had my guitar and a tiny day pack, so I stuffed the pot in the bottom of the pack, put a couple of shirts over top of the reefer, and threw a half-dozen oranges on top of that and I was ready to go.

Don Peyote gave me a handful of buttons for the trip. "Señor Mescalito will guide you." He had a lot of peyote. He had a room in his house knee deep in buttons. All these guys were gonzo. So, I ate some, walked a few blocks to I-10, and put my thumb in the air. About an hour went by, just enough time for Señor Mescalito to introduce himself.

That's when the Arizona State Police pulls up and does the usual, "Where ya goin'? What are ya doin' there? Let me see your license." Everything clicks into slooooow motion. I see my driver's license coming out of my wallet, wobbling across the space between us, into his hand. More third degree, then, "You can't hitchhike here. You gotta go to the next exit." And he's gone.

At that moment, Frog, Don Peyote and Bob come screeching around the corner, "Hey, you can't hitchhike here, you gotta go to the next exit!" "Uh...yeah." So I pile into the car and they take me to the next exit, and I'm standing there, and standing there, and Señor Mescalito says nothing. He sits. And I'm standing there...aaaand standing there, and I'm getting a little nervous. Señor Mescalito says nothing. He sits.

Then Hippy Chick walks up the ramp, and we both are thumbing. No luck. Another hour and finally an 18-wheeler comes hauling ass up the ramp. She's dancing the can-can. Ta, ta. Ta ta ta ta, ta ta, and he slams on the brakes, and me and Trucker, and Hippy Chick, and Señor Mescalito are rollin' due East. Whew! We stopped at a roadhouse juke in New Mexico for a few drinks. Trucker's putting the move on Hippy Chick, and I'm watching a pool game. The three playing pool are talking between shots about the UFOs they saw the week before, and about the upcoming nauga hunt. This was evidently the place to view the "visitors" in the West. These guys have some time on their hands, way out here. Señor Mescalito sits in the corner. The nauga hunt is a gathering in the desert where the whole town comes together with lots of food, and drink, and whatever else, and parties way into the morning. After everyone is sufficiently lubricated, it escalates into a giant brawl. All differences of opinions from the year are settled, and everyone, bruised and bloodied, returns to town to begin anew.

So, they turn to me, "Hey, come on and take a few shots." "Naw, I'm no good at pool."
"Come on, we need one more."
Well, I'd played some pool at the Club Juana. David Miller showed me the basics, but I was terrible. The champion of the scratch shot. Señor Mescalito sat, with the implication of a smile.
"OK, I'll play one."
I could do no wrong. I ran the table.
"Thank you, Gentlemen. That was fun. My ride's about to leave. See ya!"

Trucker and Hippy Chick left me out in the desert near Van Horn, Texas. Nothing. Absolutely nothing. Alone in the desert. Me, my knapsack, my guitar, and the wind blowing the little tin bell attached to my guitar case. "Ching, ching." Señor Mescalito was far away. Out in the chaparral. Every now and then, I'd feel a twinge from yesterday's ingestion of peyote, catching a glimpse of Señor Mescalito, wandering at a distance. The wind would blow and the little tin bell would sing. "Ching, ching. Ching, ching." I pulled my stocking cap down over my ears. The wind blew. "Ching, ching. Ching, ching." I stood there, flagging as the scant traffic passed. Nobody stopped. "Ching, ching." Señor Mescalito was nowhere to be seen. He had done his work and he was gone. "Ching, ching. Ching, ching." Finally, a little Winnebago camper roared past, swerved off the road, and stopped. I grabbed my stuff and ran. Took me all the way to my home in Tallahassee.

Smuggler's Cove

Going down, down to Smuggler's Cove
Going down, down to Smuggler's Cove
I might walk, I might fly, I got a serious load

Well a nickel is a nickel, and a dime is a dime
I said a nickel is a nickel, and a dime is a dime
Going down to the Cove, gonna get mine this time

Well I moved out to the county,
Got me a temporary pole
I moved out to the county
Got me a temporary pole
It ain't that I like digging, but I
Sure hate to sell my soul

Going down to the Gulf Stream,
Just to hear the Gulf breeze blow
Going down to the Gulf Stream,
I wanna hear that Gulf breeze blow
It's the sweetest song, the sweetest song I know

Well they threw me in the jailhouse,
Slammed that old jailhouse door
They threw me in the jailhouse,
They slammed that old jailhouse door
And now I can't smuggle, I can't smuggle no more

And then there's the unassuming turnip. I forget just how good a turnip can be. And then I bump into one at the market, or it hits me in the head when I'm trying to think of something different to cook. I love me some turnip greens with the root chopped into little cubes. That's some good eating. There are some places where they revere the turnip. It's featured in Asian cooking, and in France the turnip is considered a delicacy. But you know the French folks also consider chitterlings to be pretty good. I was shopping at a high-end gourmet market in Paris one time, and they had a kilo of mullet roe for sale. They were asking $150 for it. So I get back to the Gulf Coast and I'm sittin' in Panacea, Florida, munchin' on a big yellow egg sack o' redneck caviar, with a great big, gimongous splooge of Liquid Summer Hot Sauce. That roe is goood! Mullet Royale! But I diverge... Back to turnips.

Spicy Turnip Soup

1 lb turnips
3 carrots
1 sweet potato
1 large onion
1 cup rice
2 qt vegetable broth
1 cup milk
3 Tbsp Liquid Summer Hot Sauce
Salt and pepper to taste

Peel and chop the vegetables.
Throw them in the broth with the rice.
Cook covered for 20 minutes.
Puree the whole mess.
Throw it all back in the pot with the milk, Liquid
Summer Hot Sauce, salt and pepper.
Bring it slowly back up to a boil and serve.

Jefferson County is a dark corner, and to this day, it is the only county in Florida with not one single traffic light. In the '70s, a group of writers, hippies, and musicians bought some land in Jefferson County, divvied it up, and built their own homes in a small community called Peckerwood. I did not name it, but I ended up there. Legend has it that these ersatz woodworkers were kicking around possible names for this little subdivision. Since everyone was carvin' and hackin' and cuttin' and nailin', something with wood in the name would be appropriate. Names like "Yellow Wood" came up. So Larry Vickers, the guy that started the whole mess, was chasing Kathy "Crash" Craddock through the forest in amorous pursuit. They ran back and forth from one end to the other, and then they came to a giant dead pine tree. They ran around and around. Finally, Kathy stops, exclaiming, "This is not Yellow Wood. This is Peckerwood!" Not long after, I bought in.

The Peckerwood Rock Festival

That was one gig that I missed, but this is what I heard. Larry had friends all over the place. And there was a lot of excitement among the citizens of Peckerwood who envisioned a bold new social experiment. Artsy people of all types living in peace and harmony, and so on. So, Larry and company decided to share this utopia and have a few folks out to have a little party. They invited a few people, then it went viral. People came from California, Colorado, and who knows where, in hippy vans, jeeps and jalopies. The local scene got wind, and showed up in full regalia. Cars were parked in every nook and cranny, and haphazardly stretched out on both sides of the road for a long, long way. The party was at full-tilt-boogie when the cops showed up. The band was cranking it out, and the revelers were stoked. The sheriff was there to shut it down, but was having trouble getting anyone's attention. The music was loud and out of control. The musicians seemed to be in their own little world. One of the deputies, trying to get the drummer's attention, shined his flashlight in his face. The LSD had already kicked in. The drummer figured, of course, this bright light was enlightenment from God, and it was time for him to take a solo. The boogada boogada boogada was just too much for the sheriff, who then discharged his shotgun and loudly proclaimed the end of the party. When the sun came up there was an Easter egg hunt in the bushes and under the leaves for the little stashes left in haste as the party scattered like a giant flock of gooney birds. And the Peckerwoodians lived happily ever after. Well, almost.

We were living in Tallahassee when we bought four-and-a-half acres 17 miles east of town. My friends came out to help me build a shed. Actually, I helped them build a lumber shed for me to store materials that I collected to make a house. I also helped tear down a tobacco barn for a share of the two-by-fours, and tin. I scavenged an old motel for bricks, flooring, and windows. Salvaged some four-by-eight beams. Copped a huge truckload of wood from a trash pile at a lumber yard for siding. A sliding glass door turned sideways became a picture window. I loaded that ol' El Camino down, the flooring boards hanging off the back, bumpin' the road, and the front of the truck pointed to the sky. The ends of the boards sanded down to a 45-degree angle from scraping on the asphalt. I picked up lime rocks from the side of the road. I was in the salvation business.

We were paying a $100 a month for rent in town, and a $100 for the land payment. That seemed a little excessive, so Ruthie, Annie, Mary, and I decided to move into the lumber shed. The day before our son Floyd was born, we went to the hardware store to buy the box for electric hookup. Those good ol' boys took one look at long-haired dad, two little hippy children, and Mama's bout to bust, and they gave us one hell of a deal. I took the scavenged stuff and made walls and floors. It was a little cabin. Actually, it was nothing more than a shack. Soon as I began the project the truck broke down, so I was hitchhiking to town to buy nails. After the nails were used up, I'd pull the nails out of the old barn wood, straighten 'em out, and pound 'em back into the lumber. I had a big magnet that I would drag around the site where I had pulled the nails out to collect 'em. It was like *Little House on the Prairie* meets *Survivor*.

Photo: Karen Vickers

In the photo of Mary and Nemo the cat, the slanted boards behind the upright beam made a ladder into the loft. The first step jutted out and doubled as a seat, too high for a baby to climb. At the time of that photo, I had invested $400 for the cabin. I ended up paying $1800 total to build our little nest in the woods. The rest was paid in sweat and blood. The best investment I ever made.

There were no locks on the doors. I didn't have anything anyone wanted anyway. There was a wood stove for heat, a screened-in kitchen with a wood cook stove, and a bathtub in a tiny space beside the kitchen. I found a huge old rotted pine stump that was deep in the clay. I removed the remains of the stump and chiseled a big hole out of the hardpan for a privy. We carried our water for a while, until the pipes were laid from the pump, and we scratched out a pioneer living in the woods. Hard work for the whole family, but looking back, those were good times.

Photo: Karen Vickers

Annie
Photo: Diane Zielinski

Photo: Ruth Wharton

We planted jasmine upside the cabin. Now it's a shed again, and in the springtime a solid bloom covers the entire place, and fills the whole yard with wafts of sweetness. I think the jasmine holds that old shed together.

My favorite way to cook is on a wood stove. The convection in the oven makes the biscuits so nice with highlights and a depth in the browning that's absolutely gorgeous. The flavor of the wood mingling with sweet potatoes, collards, cornbread, or whatever, is like nothing else.

The summer after we moved to Peckerwood, we discovered little wild rabbiteye blueberries growing a few yards from the house. Our day started with crankin' up the cook stove, and foraging for tiny tartness to put in the pancakes covered in homemade cane syrup. I'm dyin'. Want some now!

Rabbiteye Blueberry Pancakes

2 cups whole wheat flour
1 tsp baking powder
½ tsp baking soda
½ tsp salt
1 egg
2 cups milk
2 cups rabbiteye blueberries
Sift dry ingredients.
Add milk, egg, and berries
Pour onto a hot griddle.
Flip em once.
Pour warm cane syrup all over 'em.
Makes almost enough pancakes.

Paco Reed played a little sax in Los Angeles. Didn't have a horn, but he'd show up at the jam sessions carrying a mouthpiece. He lived next door to us in Peckerwood. A dude with a truly charismatic personality, he was a frogman during the Korean War, and had tattoos all over his body before tattoos were in. Wore chinos without a belt, sandals, and no shirt, loved his tall Budweisers, Jack Daniels, and his garden. A garden right by the road. He'd be out there hoein' and plantin' and waterin.' All organic, his chickens provided fertilizer, and he worked magic. Beans, collards, tomatoes, just about everything. Scattered throughout was his marijuana. We all thought that was pretty brazen, but Paco was smoooth.

One day, sure enough, the deputy sheriff comes rollin' down the drive, nice and slow. Paco was standing there with his trusty hoe and that killer smile. Deputy stops at the garden, slowly rolls down the window, surveys the crops, and drawls, "Them's some mighty sporty 'maters you got there, Paco." He slowly rolled the window up and slowly drove away.

We Peckerwoodians considered that the first green light in Jefferson County. That was the beginning of some serious gardening. We had us a time. Things were going so well. Then Paco died. He left a beautiful wife, three sons, and Paquito in the womb. There's a fence around his grave. On the cast iron gate are the words "Paco's Garden."

Paco's Garden

There's a place where I go
Where time, it moves so slow
And I can find myself a peaceful pardon
For all the things I've done
And all the times I've run
I always seem to come to Paco's garden

Ain't no complaint, ain't no kind of patron saint
Ain't no such word as cain't in Paco's garden
Just a man with a hoe, watching the flowers grow
And that's all I know 'bout Paco's garden

I remember the day we laid the old man down
There was a dogfight and the kids were running 'round
Hell, Floyd almost fell into the hole
But after all these years
These are real, honest-to-goodness, bona fide tears
Watering the ground in Paco's garden

There's a place where I go, way down in Mexico
Muy simpático, mi amigo
And when I've done my time
And I got no more hills to climb
Just bring me back to Paco's garden

My life has had an off-kilter symmetry. It seems appropriate that I was introduced to cannabis when I was working at the Club Juana. I would smoke a little weed during the break and David Miller would kick me in the butt during the show. Little did I know that it would grow to be a lifetime relationship with the plant. A plant that would make me more aware of not only myself, but also itself. Who/what/how are we?

Peckerwood

Chicks in the Peckerwood nearly half grown
Jump on a doobie like a dog on a bone
Rockin on the porch, and layin' in the shade
Countin' all the money that cha Daddio made

Goin' down to Peckerwood, goin' on a run
Goin' down to Peckerwood to have a little fun
Goin' down to Peckerwood – and when I'm done
Gonna make a run! Gonna make a run!

Born in Peckerwood, when I was a kid
Got me a taste of a Peckerwood lid
No matter where I went, no matter what I did
I had a grin so big that I couldn't keep it hid
Goin' down to Peckerwood, goin' on a run
Goin' down to Peckerwood to have a little fun
Goin' down to Peckerwood – and when I'm done
Gonna make a run! Gonna make a run!

Photo: Bill Wharton

Needless to say, living in Peckerwood expanded my horizons. The photo above is my first ever selfie. Me and my little Hawaiian girlfriend. She was sswweeet!

I began with a half dozen Colombian seeds. I was immediately entranced. I would find myself standing in front of these little beauties not knowing how I even got there, caring for their needs. "What do y'all need today?" It was not a chore. Soon it was Hawaiian. Earlier to mature and, like I said, very sweet buds. After that it was "research." Jamaican, a very strong, pungent, spicy Indica brought to the island by East Indian servants. Great smoke, but with hermaphroditic tendencies. When those girls got horny enough they would grow different equipment, and do the do. Luckily, I caught 'em before the clouds of pollen engulfed the entire patch. Colombian Gold, the color of the sunshine. Or the Redbud, also from Colombia. Tiny little dense tight buds that will put you into next week. The Afghani, earliest to bloom and the skunkiest too. Oh, I forgot about the Panama Red. Actually, a dark purple (almost black) spicy sativa with a kick. Then there was the Thai. I had a strain of Thai that was the most amazing of all. One hit shit. Gorgeous bronze buds maturing later, between the Hawaiian and the Colombian. When the cold weather hit, the little white hairs would grow out a brilliant magenta. Sigh.

Hawaiian
Photo: Ruth Wharton

Did I mention the hybrids? The plants from the union of the Jamaican hermaphrodites and the Thai were vigorous monsters. The tallest plant I ever grew was a Black Afghani crossed with Hawaiian that reached 17 feet. The strain was called Big Mama Thornton. When mature, the lowest branches were about four feet off the ground and stretched out six feet horizontally. Strong silvery gray buds. That was some good pot! However, the hardiest, best all-round choice was the ANGA. A four-way hybrid. African Ganja crossed with the Nepalese, then crossed with a Colombian Goldbud which had been treated with colchicine, a mitotic inhibitor which produces a polyploid mutation. I got these seeds from a friend and crossed them with the Afghani to make it mature earlier. One hundred percent survival rate on cuttings. The roots made an almost impenetrable thick mat. Survives in just about any climate. Tasty, and strong!

It was easily 10, 15 degrees cooler under the canopy that was absorbing all the energy from the sun. I would take my National out among the plants in the summertime and sit beneath the "trees" and play those high sliding riffs. I heard the research that plants respond to classical and also Hawaiian music. My theory is they feel the vibrations of the high-pitched violins and the Hawaiian guitars. I think they are affected by the glissandos and dissonances from the slide. It seemed to work because those puppies jumped. The legend grew like a 17-foot hybrid. After all these years, I still remember. All of it. Wow!

Come to find out, cannabis cures cancer. It's also used to treat multiple sclerosis, Parkinson's disease, post-traumatic stress disorder, ADHD, epilepsy, glaucoma, pain, drug and alcohol addiction, and seizures, to name a few.

Delta 9 Blues

Sometimes I need a little something for my mind
I said sometimes, people
I need a little something for my mind
Talkin' about reefer, Baby, I just want a little Delta 9

Well the river come a rollin'
All the way down to the sea
Bring a little reefer home for you and me
I said the river come a rollin' on down to the sea
Bring a little reefer back home for you and me
But what it is, gonna have to wait and see

Sometimes I need a little something for my mind
Sometimes I need a little something for my mind
Talkin' about a reefer, to ease my worried mind

The most dangerous trip I ever took? It was not the time I hitchhiked out to Tucson. It was not the high-speed chase ending with a 357-caliber bullet whizzing over my head. No, it was the time I went on the quest for the perfect shit. Yes, shit. I was a connoisseur of shit. Chicken shit, cow shit, horse shit, rabbit shit, you name it. Shit! I wanted the best compost I could get for my babies. The only way to do that is make it yourself, so here ya go. Across the highway from my place is a 5,000-acre plantation and hunting reserve. Veeery exclusive. You could bring yer wife and she could hang out like Scarlett did, while you're out baggin' wild turkeys, quail, dove, deer, or whatever, for a mere $500 a day. They used mule-drawn carriages for the hunting parties, and since it was practically right next door, it proved to be a valuable source. Mule shit is cool shit. So, I, the connoisseur, in my element, would clean out the piles of manure.

They were happy for this peasant to rid them of the "soil." To kick it up a notch, I went to the coast and got a couple of 55-gallon drums full of fish guts. I had been saving wood ashes, and I bought some lime to "sweeten the pot" as it were. But for the pièce de résistance I needed crab meal. That's shells and guts ground up to bits, and dried. Very intense nutrients, and minerals, and very bad if you happen to be a nematode. I loaded up a barrel in the back of my El Camino and headed back down to the coast. I tell you what. Fifty-five gallons of hot steamin' funk will make a man happy. I felt like celebrating so I took some time to cruise down to Apalachicola and have a few beers. A few turned into many. I closed down the bar, slipped it down into overdrive and raged up Highway 98 toward Peckerwood. Now in 1959, they designed the overdrive for the El Camino kind of like one of those Chinese finger puzzles. It was activated by the accelerator. When you backed off the gas pedal, the car was free-wheeling. Push on the gas pedal, and it was full-on go. Plus, the 1959 had those wings in the back that lifted the rear end. Put a good load in the back and it was like nothing was back there. Like a sleigh ride to hell, that heavy I-beam construction shot down the road with a load of funky crab, a huge inertia barreling into the night. I was lit. I got a ways up the road, and there was an RV pulled over with lights flashing. I pulled over, got out, walked over to the vehicle and asked, "Y'all need some help?" And then I passed out. I woke with the dew and a hangover. The RV was nowhere to be seen. About a third of the crab meal had blown out the back. Those folks broken down by the side of the road probably saved my life. This is the dumb-ass part. But that ain't the half of it. There's plenty more where that came from. Shit!

The Perfect Shit

Two pickup truck loads mule shit
110 gal fish heads, fins, tails, and entrails
35 gal crab meal (or more if you can get it home)
10 gal wood ashes
Lime to taste

Make a huge layer cake of the ingredients.
First a layer of manure.
Then the fish.
Sprinkle a layer of lime.
Then the crab meal.
Then the ashes.
Repeat until the ingredients are all on the pile.
Cover and leave it for a couple of months.
After it cooks down, uncover the pile and enjoy.

I Bait My Hook by the Light of the Moon

Flying under the radar, I've been huggin' the coast
Just over the limit, I've been diagnosed
It ain't no gimmick, it's only a tune
I bait my hook by the light of the moon

I got a bad disposition, I'm a mean old man
Livin' in the shadow, I got a secret plan
It ain't no evil, it's only a tune
I bait my hook by the light of the moon

It's a tough situation, it's a shame and a sham
But on a good night of fishing, you can see me jam
It ain't my condition, it's only a tune
I bait my hook by the light of the moon

Now you don't understand it, you can't find the thread
All the critics have panned it,
I'm just making some bread
Makin' out like a bandit with a dance and a tune
I bait my hook by the light of the moon

The guitar on this song is a yellow TV Model double cutaway 1959 Les Paul going through a 1948 Fender Pro and a 1956 Vibrolux.

Liquid Summer Bloody Mary
1 cup tomato juice
1 Tbsp Liquid Summer Hot Sauce
1 tsp horseradish
Dash of celery salt
1 tsp Worcestershire sauce
2 tsp lemon juice
Couple shots of vodka
Mix ingredients together and pour into a glass of ice.

I was rolling in more ways than one. But I had a sense way down deep that something was not working. I was great at growing things, but I was not a very good outlaw. I was looking for the benefits of this wonderful, amazing herb, and I also wanted to share it with all my friends. I remember one Christmas, when I left the house with a quarter pound of fresh buds, riding in my bright red El Camino sleigh, stopping to visit friends. At the end of the day, all the presents had been delivered and my sack was empty. "Ho, Ho, Ho"! Those days were balls to the walls. It was just a matter of time before... well you know. Not a huge surprise when the knock came at the door. Six cars, each filled to the brim with the Big Bend Narcotics Task Force, just to bust little ol' me. All part of the drug war started by Richard Nixon and continued by Ronald Reagan "to target Hippies and Blacks." A war that still rages. If that ain't enough, a few weeks later it got worse. A lot worse.

The Muck Brothers

Y'all don't know the half of it. To tell this part of the story I will have to back up a bit. A few years prior, there had been another bust in Peckerwood. That was when the legends started. The deputies were saying that they needed chain saws to remove the plants. The charges were dropped. However, that ended my growing operation in the backyard. We could count on a yearly visit of a helicopter hovering very low over my house and garden. To continue my research, I had to move the ops elsewhere.

Back when I was serenading my Hawaiian beauties in my backyard, my friend and neighbor, Dan, came over and asked to see my plants. Funny thing was they were in plain view, but he didn't see them. I'd cleared a little circle that was surrounded by saplings and brush. The small trees were about 10 feet high. I thought that should be plenty to hide the virgins. Wrong. By June the reefer was stretching out over the trees, and by August you could sit in the cabin and watch the top four feet of buds waving in the wind. "Hellooooo"! But nobody ever saw them. When Dan asked to see them, we walked across the yard into the woods and stopped. Although he said nothing, his face was like, "So, where are they?" Then he looked down. Covering the ground were giant bright yellow marijuana leaves. Then he looked up.

Dan and I began planning a clandestine horticulture enterprise. First, we started some ANGA seedlings indoors. While they were growing, we perused topo maps to find the most remote areas in Jefferson County. We looked for places surrounded by water or swamp that were high enough to grow.

We found an outcropping of lime rock and chert in the middle of a swamp protected by water, muck, and cottonmouth moccasins. Swampside. It was a prehistoric native destination for making tools. While digging we found lots of chips along with spear points and arrowheads. We got to be good friends with the cottonmouths that lived there. Moc One, and Moc Two. The first time we went to Swampside, we met them. As we were walking down a path, we came upon Moc One, a healthy snake about three feet long all coiled up in the middle of the path. We stopped suddenly and waited. Slow as molasses, Moc One uncoiled and slowly moved from the path, taking his time. After a few minutes the path was clear to pass. That's when I looked down, and right next to my leg was Moc Two. Moc Two was a huge snake, and she was coiled with her head back ready to strike. A guard snake. Cool! We never had a problem at Swampside. We also found a little canal dug to drain the swamp for a road. It was six feet wide and three or four feet deep. About 50 yards into the swamp there was a little hill of sand dredged from the canal. The Canal Zone. We spent months clearing and preparing the ground. We would return home, exhausted and completely covered in muck. We were the Muck Brothers. Then we brought in the fertilizer. Bags of chicken manure loaded to the top of Dan's truck. On top of the fertilizer we put my canoe. We loaded the canoe with the bags and pushed it down the canal in the pitch-black night. There was just enough room to slide the boat down the canal. Wading through the cold, black, waist-deep water was pretty creepy, not knowing what kind of critters might be swimming in there. Not long after, we brought in eight-foot plants that had been under lights for 18 hours a day. The short days of winter freaked them out so bad that they instantly started making huge buds. In April there were buds as long as your arm.

We had a jump on the market. Then six cars completely filled to the brim pulled up to my house, and you know the rest. Almost.

At that point I was ready to quit growing, but I had loose ends to tie up at the Canal Zone. We harvested everything putting the plants in large tarps like giant burritos. However, they were so heavy that we could not lift them. So we divided them up into smaller bags and tossed them in the back of the truck. On the way out, a wildlife officer stopped us. He said, "I'd like to check what's in the back." Dan said, "OK." When he got around to the back of the truck, Dan turned to me and casually asked, "Shall we go?" "Sure." And the race was on.

We were winning. Through swamps and monstrous puddles, deep ruts, through planted pines with just enough room for the truck to squeeze. We lost him. But then we turned down a cul de sac. We tossed the bags and I was running for the woods. That's when I heard the shot and a 357 slug whizzing right over my head. He shouted, "FREEZE ASSHOLE!" And it did.

This was all pretty scary. However, the scariest part, the part that really frightened me, was not the high-speed chase. It was not the bullet whizzing overhead. It was not this tough guy with mirrored shades and USMC tattooed to his arm aiming his pistol at my head. The scariest part was that he was shaking like a leaf with his finger on the trigger. That. Was. Scary. But y'all still don't know the half of it.

Outlaw Blues

Somebody came and dropped my name
Somebody came and dropped my name
I'm the one everybody gonna blame

Now the county's on my back
Now the county's on my back
They all came down to my little old shack

The judge was busy adjudicatin'
The judge was busy adjudicatin'
I had to take me a little vacation

Took me down to the county farm
Took me down to the county farm
Me and the sheriff, arm in arm

Won't somebody please tell my woman
Won't somebody please tell my woman
I cain't say when, I'll be comin' home

I got nothing left to lose
I got nothing left to lose
Singing these old outlaw blues

Instant Key Lime Banana Ice Cream

6 frozen bananas, chopped
3 key limes
3 oz plain yogurt
¼ cup maple syrup
1 tsp vanilla
Juice the limes and dump all the ingredients into a
food processor. Delish!

The state's attorney was very happy. "We'll put this guy away for a year and a half." I knew I was going down. I needed a break from the stress. If I was gonna do time like that, I needed to blow it out before I went away. So I went to the beach, dropped acid, opened a bottle of wine, and watched the sunset. It cleared the cobwebs, but it gave me a hangover. So to cure the queasies, I'm rolling through Apalachicola, smoking a joint, looking for breakfast, and a deputy sees me and pulls me over. I'm wearing a straw fishing hat with a green visor in the front with a jack of hearts and a small piece of tinfoil holding a few blotters stuck in the brim. Also, I'm wearing the loudest Hawaiian shirt ever, with raspberry drawstring pants. He takes one look at me and says, "You are under arrest!" So he's searching the van and he calls the office to check my license out. After a while he says, "The computer is down, so I'm gonna let you go. But you know smoking that stuff can ruin yer whole weekend." I agreed, "Thank you, Sir." In the period of about month, I almost became a three-time loser. It was time for me to change my ways. I never planted cannabis again.

Sixty days in the Jefferson County jail, plus three years of probation. That's what I received for growing the cure for cancer. Given what we know now about why cannabis is illegal, I consider my small time in jail was spent as a political prisoner. (For an historical view of cannabis see the link at the end of this book to *The Emperor Wears No Clothes*). But I learned how to play Tonk, and Dirty Hearts (the deck was marked). In the two months I was there, I won only one hand at cards. But I taught a few of the guys how to read, and I got a glimpse of just how bad it is for some, and how fortunate I am. Wrote some tunes and read a lot of books. I even got to swing a blade one day on the "chain gang." I had my street cred. Plus, we had some outrageous parties. No beer, no wine, no whiskey, no marijuana. Just some losers, some very unfortunate folks who were in the wrong place at the wrong time, some innocent and some who had done some bad things and got caught. All telling jokes and talkin' trash all night long. And we sang. Within a week, I was a trustee. I had the run of the place. Plus, I cooked for the fellas, taking a huge can of beans and turning it into a chef-d'oeuvre. A masterpiece. Just like Mama would do. There were some good times among the bad. A vacation of sorts, but I missed opening for John Lee Hooker. I also had a gig booked to be the backup band for Bo Diddley, and at the last minute it looked as though I might lose my good time, thereby also missing that date. I was devastated. It was Good Friday. The lowest I have ever been. Some of the longest days of my life. The time was creeping by. Sitting on my bed, trying to figure out how to make rope out of a blanket. Little did I know, it would be all up from there. Then the intercom blared, "Wharton! Grab your stuff and come up front!"
I was free!

Des Haricots de Chef de Sauce en Prison
(Jailhouse Beans)

1 gal can baked beans
1 16 oz can tomatoes, diced (include the juice)
4 large onions, diced
3 green peppers, diced
4 Tbsp garlic powder
1 lb bacon, diced
¼ cup honey
½ bottle of hot sauce
Salt and pepper
Sauté the onions, garlic, bacon, and green peppers.
Add the other ingredients and bake.

Bo shows up at the gig for sound check. Takes one look at the band, and with trepidation, asks, "Is this the band?" Our little trio of hayseeds replied, "Yup! We're the band!" And with more trepidation, "Well, OK then." After 15 minutes of jammin', Bo asks, "You guys got a tape recorder? I wanna get some of this down." It worked! With a 15-minute warm up, we played four hours of raging rock 'n roll. Less than a week before, I was sitting in a jail cell. Needless to say, I was ready to rock. And believe me, that ain't even half, it ain't even a quarter of the story.

Photo: Mickey Adair

Butternut Papaya Bisque

1 lb of squash steamed
½ lb fresh papaya, chopped into chunks
1 pint fresh organic almond milk
Dusting of ground nutmeg
Put everything in a blender.
Heat and serve.

I was on the way up, but not everything I tried worked. Those times were extremely difficult. Jail time, no matter how small, puts a hurtin' on a family, emotionally and financially. I was taking any kind of gig I could get. Restaurants, pubs, whatever. I had a solo engagement at Sloppy Joe's in Key West, playin the Bloody Mary set. It was snakebit from the start. Halfway through the week, I left Key West like a scalded dog.

I played the first set of the day. I arrived as they opened the shutters. Only me, the bartender, and a half-dozen heavy boozers were in there. Actually, it was not a solo gig. I had an accompanist. There was a multi-talented guy playing the skill saw and switching to hammer and nails sitting in while I was doing my thing. I was pulling out all the stops. I tried every trick I knew. I even played some music, but it just was not to be. The owner at that time was Big Jim. Big Jim was a big biker guy who later succumbed to the AIDS epidemic. When they cleaned out his house, they filled up three big garbage bags with Bic lighters. Big Jim be smokin' that shit. The day I met Big Jim, I was finally getting a little something goin'.

Word got out about this crazy singer/songwriter, and I had a little crowd listening. I did this percussion thing where I'd take a pair of drumsticks and tap on everything on stage, then move into the audience and tap on tables, glasses, bald heads, whatever was there just like I'd do when I pulled out my Mama's pots and pans back when I was little. I would usually end up behind the bar tapping out melodies on the bottles. When I went behind the bar, Big Jim said, "Fire that guy!"

So the general manager went to Bill Blue (who was booking the entertainment) and said, "You need to fire Wharton." Bill replied, "I'm not gonna fire Wharton." So the next day the GM politely said, "It's not working out." I believe he actually did me a favor. But that's not the half of it. That was the second time I was fired by Sloppy's. From time to time, I have thought about going back and landing a job at Sloppy Joe's one more time so that I can get fired for a much better reason.

I got ahold of some datil peppers and planted the seeds, never thinkin' I would actually sell peppers. Around that time, I was growing something that brought more of a financial yield. However, I love hot peppers and would make my own sauce from the garden using jalapeños for a heat source. Immediately realizing the unique character of the datils, I began experimenting with different recipes. Not only is the flavor a unique, robust, sweet funk, the heat is a creeper burn, coming up slow, from the bottom. The full effect of the capsicum takes about 15 seconds to arrive. First you have this thick complex flavor, then after about 10 seconds you feel the initial burn. About five seconds later, the warmth of the mids pops through.

And this last little bit is what swells like a symphony in your mouth after you finish. Those 10 seconds before the heat arrives gives you all time to taste the other ingredients. A compassionate habanero.

Most of the datil sauces out there are like a spicy ketchup. What I aimed for was something different. Somewhere between a Louisiana hot sauce and a Caribbean salsa. That's where Florida is at, geographically. Sooo, why not chunky veggies chopped into a pepper-vinegar base? I wanted a personal stash of excellent flavor.

Well, I made some sauce and it was gone in no time. After they tasted it, my friends wanted some. I would make a gallon, and it would be history within a week. If all these people were gonna come to my house and eat up all my sauce, I was gonna bottle it up and sell it to 'em.

I bought a pressure cooker and a rototiller. I got a semi-truckload of mushroom compost dumped in my yard, and I was feeling good. That was a big ol' pile of doo-doo. Y'all know how I like doo-doo. I grew a bunch of datils, made some sauce, and called it Liquid Summer. And Brothers and Sisters, I'm here to tell you: Liquid Summer changed my life!

Now, I had done my time; however, I was still on probation. After two and a half years, I was over it. My lawyer took some Liquid Summer to show the judge. The judge said, "Where can I get some of that hot sauce?" It worked!

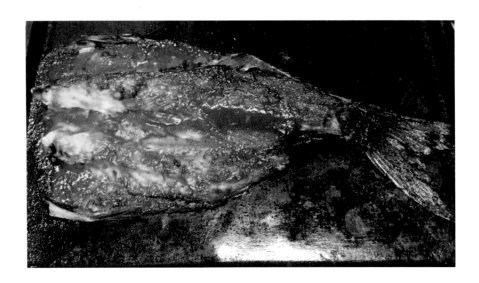

Liquid Summer BBQ Mullet

Spray the pan with oil, broil the mullet, finish it off
under the broiler with your favorite BBQ sauce, and
Liquid Summer Hot Sauce. Best served cold, but who's
gonna wait for that? Make a bunch. Don't get no
better than a late-night cold BBQ mullet snack.

Photo: Jeff Weil

I was a regional act. I played from South Carolina to Key West. Tobacco Road in Miami was a regular rockin' gig. Skipper's Smokehouse in Tampa was another. Paddy O'Toole's Four-for-One Night in Mobile was another wild ass gig. Melbourne was also a favorite stop. It was a place where everything felt comfortable.

The most laid-back place on the East Coast of Florida, with a happening local scene, Brevard County always had a hold on me, so playing the Wine Gallery was like coming home. I got together with blues DJ, Gary Zajac who would become a lifelong friend of mine as well. I'd take my guitar to the radio station and jam until Mr. Z would fire up his hot rod and burn out of there.

Meanwhile, in Orlando, a boogie-woogie storm was brewing. King Snake Records began releasing recordings of blues artists. Kenny Neal, Lucky Peterson, Reverend Billy Wirtz, Root Boy Slim, and Noble "Thin Man" Watts, were a few who recorded albums there. Somehow, I managed to wrangle my way onto the label. The man at King Snake was Bob Greenlee. He was a musician/gourmand/sportsman and he liked the hot sauce, and the culinary blues I was putting down. So, Bob produced *The Sauce Boss,* and I became part of the King Snake family. Good times. I would end up recording five albums at King Snake. It worked!

I'm Cookin'

Yeah, I'm cookin', I'm cookin' tonight
Yes, I'm cookin', I'm cookin' tonight
Me and my Baby, we got the stove just right

Your stove's so hot, I can't stand the heat
You cooked my cornbread, you 'qued my meat
My brownie's in your oven, and I got my red beans on
The way you cook it, Baby, you can call me solid gone
We got the groceries, Baby, we got the recipe
Let's make something, Baby, just you and me

Yes, we're cookin' – we're cookin' with gas
Yeah, we're cookin', Child – we're cookin' with gas
I'm about to cook for a sweet little yes yes yes

You know you got me, Baby, at a steady rolling boil
I said you got me, Baby, at a steady rolling boil
I better eat that honey – I don't want it to spoil!

Yeah, I'm cookin', I'm cookin' tonight
Yes, I'm cookin', I'm cookin' tonight
Me and my Baby we got the stove just right

I started giving my audience a taste of my hot sauce. Liquid Summer had legs, and it was walking briskly out the door. After they tasted a sample on a chip or cracker, they laid their money down. People began calling me the Sauce Boss. It was all coming together. At the sessions for *The Sauce Boss* album, I met Kenny Neal's parents, Raful and Shirley Neal. Raful was laying down tracks of his Baton Rouge swamp blues, while Shirley was in the kitchen making gumbo, and I was watching. Right then I realized that Liquid Summer would make a gumbo jump and shout! Yes. Shirley's Louisiana gumbo recipe combined with that creeper burn, made a very distinctive gumbo. Hmm...so on December 31, 1989, I made gumbo for my audience.

Here's what I did different though: I gave it away for free. It worked.

Photo: Joe Sekora

Photo: Ruth Wharton

Gumbo

1 ½ cups flour
1 cup oil
1 chicken, cooked and deboned
1 gal of chicken stock
2 large onions, chopped
2 large green peppers, chopped
Liquid Summer Hot Sauce to taste (I use a whole bottle)
1 lb smoked sausage
2 medium zucchini
1 lb okra
1 lb of shrimp
1 pt of oysters
1 lb of crawfish tails

Make a roux: mix flour into hot oil. Cook on high, stirring constantly until brown. Sauté onions and green peppers in the roux. Add the chicken and chicken stock, bring to a boil, then simmer down. Slice and add: smoked sausage, zucchini, and okra. After the okra is done (about 30-60 min), turn up the heat, and throw the shrimp, oysters, and crawdads in there. Add salt and Liquid Summer Hot Sauce to taste. Boil for a couple minutes, till the seafood is barely cooked. Serve over rice. Feeds 8-12 people.

Liquid Summer Hot Sauce

The Sauce Boss

I'm a Sauce Boss sure is hot and good
I'm a Sauce Boss sure is hot and good
It'll make ya feel better than you thought you could

Put it on your breakfast, on your dinner too
You can shake my sauce all over your barbeque
I'm a Sauce Boss
Sure is hot and good
It'll make ya feel better than you thought you would

Everybody that tries my sauce
Is back for more and more
I'm just trying to tell ya, Baby
This here is the score
Just one taste will have you running
Back into the store
Everybody that's tried it gonna tell you that's for sure
I'm a Sauce Boss
Sure is hot and good

If you got neuritis, neuralgia too
You know my sauce will cure what is ailing you
I'm a Sauce Boss
Sure is hot and good
It'll make ya feel better than you thought you could

Cricketers Blues Club Bordeaux, France 1992
BW, John "JB" Babich, Dennis Everheart, Louis "Jiggs" Walker

The Sauce Boss album got us hooked up on a circuit in the Northeast, and licensing deals in Europe. This led to a European release of *South of the Blues* on Virgin Records. We were going to France two or three times a year. We played the New Morning jazz club in Paris a few times, a Napoleonic opera house turned rock club in Montpelier, a cathedral in Rouen, a Roman amphitheater near Nice. That was a cool gig. They called me L'Homme Que Explode Très Grand et Avec Beaucoup de Feu et Bruit (The Exploding Man)!

We did the Lionel Hampton Room at the Hotel Meridien in Paris for two weeks. This hotel had five restaurants, a sushi bar, their own bakery and butcher shop. At their high-end eatery there were no prices on the menu. So little ol' Cornbread is in the kitchen, 'splaining how to make roux to the chefs with the *tall* hats. "No, it's not the color of butter, it's the color of that bean pot over there." A far cry from Peckerwood. We got to where we would take as few clothes as possible so we could bring wine back with us. Loading up at the cave in Burgundy, after the Blues de Bourgogne Festival, I was sitting at the airport waiting to fly home with cases stacked waist high. Two cases of Burgundy in the belly of the plane, and a case under each arm. Boarding the plane was a trip in itself. "Excuse me. Pardon, Monsieur. Ooops, I'm so sorry."

And the cheese! The stinkier the better. In the duty-free stocking up at the last minute before the flight, smelling the options. "Hmm...stinky tennis shoes... um...dirty underwear, so hard to decide." Upon my opening the overhead on arrival, everyone on the plane turned to see what the hell was that. That, my friends, was the good ol' days when flying was fun. Of course, while in Bordeaux, it's a gas to exchange tokens of appreciation. It's likely to become a gift off, parlaying into a gifting frenzy. "Merci for the hot sauce. You must try a bottle of my sparkling wine." "Oh, thank you so much, here have a copy of my new album," and on and on.

Majic John Jones, BW, and Big Jim Jenness
Photo: Ruth Wharton

When Virgin Records released *South of the Blues*, we did a month in France, playing nonstop all over the place. We started with a week in Nancy and covered the entire country in 30 days. The best part of traveling anywhere is when you get to know the people and share their love of food and drink, but in France... well you know. In Nancy, we were treated with a meal before each show. Generally, a meal prepared in a home with the local cuisine. That's when you taste the home-style improvisations which have evolved into traditions. That's when you taste the little secret recipes only the locals know.

That's when I tasted the Vipère. Making moonshine is illegal in France; however, if you've got a few orchards of unsold plums and can find a licensed itinerant distiller you can still enjoy the Eau de Vie. So, this Sauce Boss enthusiast invited us to a clandestine rendezvous to taste his stash of moonshine. We sat around the table and tasted the Mirabelle, made from a small plum. Then we had the apple and a few more from his cabinet. Then he brought it out. Here's how they make it. The farmer first takes apples and distills them into shine. Then he goes to the woods and finds a tiny pit viper about a foot long. He puts the snake in a bottle and then pours the boiling shine over the snake and fills the bottle. He puts it up in the cabinet for a few months, making a tincture out of the snake. The alkaloids from the poison come out into the moonshine and the drink becomes "medicine." It is used as a cold remedy. I tasted half a shot. Much stronger than whiskey. Qualitatively stronger. It's a different animal. It's the Vipère! Those French guys will eat just about anything, as long as it's cooked right.

For the recording of *South of the Blues*, Carey Bell joined us for a session and a few gigs. When he looked at you with those pools of emotion, it would melt your heart.

Liquid Summer Cocktail Sauce

Two cups ketchup
Juice of a lemon
1 Tbsp horseradish (or more)
¼ cup Liquid Summer Hot Sauce (or more)

Stateside, one of my favorite gigs was Margaritaville in Key West. We'd spend a week basking and swimming by day, playing music until early morning, and partying until daybreak. My money was no good anywhere on the Island. A very large time was had, however, I'm so glad those days of excess are long gone. Then there was the time at the Margaritaville in New Orleans, when I met Jimmy Buffett. After we played a killer first set, he and Michael Utley and some of the folks from Margaritaville Records made a beeline to the stage.

Here's the conversation.

He began: "Hey Boss!"

"Hey Boss!"

"Man, this is the best band I've seen in a long time."

"Can I quote you on that, Jimmy"?

"...This is the best bar band I've seen in a while."

"Cool"!

"You know everybody wants to be me, but I'd rather open up a bait store and be you! You can play at my place as long as you want." That was the beginning of a mutual admiration society.

When I first heard a Buffett tune, I was impressed by the attitude and the satire. He nailed that. But I was not like some of his fans with the Hawaiian shirts, crazy glasses, and a full bar in the trunk of their car. Then he wrote *I Will Play For Gumbo*. The song with a verse about the Sauce Boss. I believe the quality of his music took a giant leap forward at that time. I was rapidly becoming a Parrothead. Joking aside, thank you Mr. Buffett for the shout out. It has been a huge boost to me, and I must say that your performance at the Casa Marina during the Meeting of the Minds in 2015 was one of the best shows I've ever seen. Congratulations.

Kino Song
The Full Moon was a Half Shell when a very Sloppy
Captain Tony Hornblower flipped like a Bottle Cap
from the Rooftop of his Backyard Pier House into the
Blue Lagoon. Pepe Siboney's Parrot Whistled at the
Bull from his Hideaway down by The Wharf and all he
said was...BABALOU!

One of these days and it won't be long
I'm gonna sing me a different song
Talk about a man paying his dues
I just gotta buy me a pair of shoes

Hey look how thin my Kinos are
I just walked down from Sloppy's bar
Came down from The Wharf – it ain't too far
Hey, look how thin my Kinos are

Early in the morning 'bout a half past noon
Couldn't make it dude, it's just too soon
I been living on a rock about the size of a dime
I just can't seem to find the time

I said look how thin my Kinos are
I just came down from Sloppy's bar
I came down from The Wharf – it ain't too far
Look how thin my Kinos are

Came all the way from Alabam
I just wanna see Jimmy Buffett jam
All dressed up and I'm fit to kill
Just got thrown out o' Margaritaville

Look how thin my Kinos are
I just walked down from Sloppy's bar
I came down from the Wharf -- it ain't too far
Hey, look how thin my Kinos are

For years, I was spooning out gumbo to good folks all over the place, and putting heart and soul into the music. That should have been enough, but there was something missing. So, I started the non-profit Planet Gumbo.

Photo: Ruth Wharton

In 2002, I took my music and gumbo to a homeless shelter and did my thing. I realized just how much you can get back when you do something for someone who can never repay you. It's still a two-way street. Like those good ol' boys who cut me some slack at the hardware store when they saw my situation. Like all those years of favors I have received when folks helped me down the road. Since then I've played and cooked at homeless shelters all over the country. Guess I've been returning the favor. When you actually go to a shelter, you realize how many good people live there: war veterans, families, and children, and folks who are handicapped. There's so much good in the world, but some folks need to get "woke" to what's truly goin' on.

BW, Justin Headley and John Hart jamming at a homeless shelter
Photo: Ruth Wharton

When I was a kid I wore hand-me-down clothes to school. When I complained, my father quoted Mahatma Gandhi. "I cried because I had no shoes, then I met a man who had no feet..."

I carried this story around in the back of my mind for over fifty years. Then one day I'm playing and cooking for The Community For Creative Non-Violence, a homeless shelter in Washington DC. In this shelter 1300 homeless clients are housed three blocks from The Mall. Getting ready for the show I was fretting about my old worn-out shoes. When I got to the gig there was a man in a wheelchair sitting in the front row. His ankles were bandaged where his feet had just been amputated. This guy, listening to my music, sitting in a homeless shelter, with no feet, had the biggest smile in the whole room. I played my heart out, with tears in my eyes. I still wear those shoes. I've resoled them three times and will never throw them out even though they are shabby with torn leather. I just polish them up once in a while and feel thankful.

That's How It Feels

Some people don't know
Some people don't care
Some people need to go back to school
And learn how to share
Too mean and nasty
To throw a dog a bone
That's how it feels to live without a home

It's a rotten crime
In the first degree
Some people use all their time
Takin' it away from me
Every day you see it
Right on the street
That's how you feel when you ain't got nothing to eat

Some people are wealthy
With the finest clothes
They the last to help me
When I almost froze
With the howlin' wind
Rippin' at my throat
That's how it feels when you haven't got a coat

Come on now Brother, Sister too
You know there's plenty
Plenty for me and you
Just take one minute
See my point of view
Put one foot in a homeless shoe

"He's awake!"
That's what she said, but the tone in the nurse's voice said, "He's alive!"
Then the hustle of attendants began.
"Mr. Wharton, if you can hear me, nod your head."
Nods.
"Are you in pain?"
Nods.
"Would you like something for the pain?"
Nods vigorously!!!!
After counting down from 100, and making it to 80 or so, my memories were put into a blender set to puree for a few seconds. Chopped and diced, they came back in a slush of images. Everyone smiling, "You did it!" Ruthie saying, "You made it!" Then nothing. The clock on the wall of the Intensive Care Unit trying to fool me, clicking each second as if it was really a second. I know that every second was streeeetched out to be half a minute. Flashing on that Muddy Waters song, "Minutes go like hours, hours go like days." Where is he? I pushed the button a long, long time ago. Doesn't he realize I'm in serious pain? The joys of morphine. Three tubes inserted into my chest. A cut, stitched back together where my sternum was split in half, my ribs jacked apart, and my sternum stapled back together again. In and out of consciousness. The endless poking and prodding, the grilled cheese sandwich drenched in butter delivered to me for lunch three days after the operation, "This is probably not for me." No sleep. Wake up for your vitals. The pills. The first sneeze. The dozing, the waking, everything mashed together. Through this discombobulated haze emerged a crystal-clear vision. It was like a dream, but it was more than that.

Everything is dark. The Sun, a smudge in the sky, not bright enough to light anything, but bright enough to provide the time of day, says noon. Fires are everywhere. Always a half a dozen boys gathered around each little source of warmth, dealing, trading, arguing about a piece of nothing, which is the world to whoever these people are. The feral boy jumps his BMX through the rubble, avoiding the piles of devastation, scrapping his way to the other side on an errand. The boy's face is covered with dirt and grime, his homemade clothes in tatters. Pillars of smoke and debris barf from chimneys of the factories. Loud crashes of indeterminate explosions punctuate the clatter of hard-scrabble, fourth-world existence of all the boys. Everyone over 16 is either in the military or in prison. Unless you're one of THEM. It was They, all dressed immaculately and spouting braggadocio jingo lingo, who changed everything. They brought back the first industrial revolution. "It's only a step backward in the progression. When we reach the beginning, everything will be so much better." Meanwhile, They have all the keys to the grid. The boys do not. He hook slides behind a pile of garbage to watch a brightly lit trolley filled with 10 to 12-year-old girls, freshly scrubbed till their cheeks look like rouge. The girls are all singing a Victorian children's song. "Merrily, merrily, merrily, merrily," ad infinitum. They make the turn and the song decrescendos into nothing. They are THEM. Across the street, a few of THEM are on the sidewalk outside a bustling eating establishment. They are having a spirited discussion of huge import. Inside the place, They are raucously doing their own brand of business.

The They on the sidewalk are pouring over a large paper diagram of widgets, and gizmos and quaint 19th century drawings. One of THEM loudly pontificates, "The Seminole Indians were the greatest mariners the world has ever seen, but they never made any money at it."

No, this was not a dream. It was a vision of the future.

After decades of excess, I had hit the wall with a couple of heart attacks and a quadruple bypass. Heavy drinking, partying all night, extreme gourmandizing around the world, and the fast food on the road caught up with me. Again, y'all don't know the half of it.

I realized that if I didn't change my ways, I would not be around. I changed my diet, shed 50 pounds, and had more stamina and focus. And I had a new vision of the world around me. It was like seeing the nuts and bolts of instant karma, finally seeing the implications of what I was putting into my body. So now, I try to eat a whole-foods, plant-based, low-fat thing. That's a difficult thing to do while travelling, but I do what I can. Sometimes I'll splurge, but generally, I try to avoid meat, oil, and dairy as much as possible. The difference in the way I feel is incredible. If you are curious about how I got healthier, check out the links at the end of this book. For a quick view, watch the movie, *Forks Over Knives*.

I Broke My Heart

I broke my heart all by myself
Came so natural, didn't need no help
I broke my heart, half in two
Now there's nothing left for me to do

It's a dirty shame what I have done
I'll take the blame for what's to come
I'm on the floor, I'm in a heap
I can't eat and I can not sleep

Can't see tomorrow, too far away
There's only sorrow from yesterday
Look at the time, come creepin' by
It's all my fault and now it's my turn to cry

I can't tell you why I feel so bad
This is the worse I ever had
There ain't no word for this kind of pain
There's nothing left for me but a scream

I broke my heart all by myself
Came so natural, didn't need no help
I broke my heart, half in two
Now there's nothing left for me to do

Liquid Summer Gazpacho

2 cups tomato juice
2 stalks celery
1 cucumber
1 green pepper
2 cloves garlic, minced
1 avocado
1 medium onion
1 cups ripe green olives
2 Tbsp Liquid Summer Hot Sauce
Chop veggies into 1-inch pieces.
Process the veggies for a few seconds.
Add tomato juice and Liquid Summer and chill.

I carry a little kitchen in a suitcase, a grill and a soup pot, spices, and utensils, and I have a pantry in my van. I'm able to throw down a gourmet spread wherever I land. I'm not at the mercy of the fast food cartel.

I'm loving me some nomad life. I get in and out, and nobody gets hurt. "No mad". I've got friends from all over crisscrossing paths as we go. After decades of travel, one day you wake up, look around, and calculate. The good times against the bad, the half full against the half empty, the fat gigs against the skinny little jobs, the magic against the mire, and you realize that it's mainly in your head and your heart. From the Beatles to the Bible, there's agreement. Love is the answer.

And spaghetti! One of my favorite things to cook, it can be made easily wherever you are. Like here in the Florida Keys on a picnic table.

If you have one pot you can do it all from scratch, or you can buy ready-made sauce and doctor it up to make a hardy meal. The thing that brings it all together is Liquid Summer Hot Sauce. Just a couple of tablespoons of Liquid Summer bridges the gap between the ingredients with datil pepper flavor.

Take a head of garlic, a medium onion, sweet or hot peppers, mushrooms, ground beef, or mussels, or vegan crumbles, tomato sauce, Liquid Summer Hot Sauce, oregano, summer savory, and parsley. Enjoy.

And then...

I'm lying face down on a marble slab for the better part of an hour, soaking in the dense aromatic steam, with sweat running in rivulets off my body and into my eyes, the heat and humidity cooking me into a dreamlike state. The masseur slaps me on the back, WHAM! Then he begins the most intense massage and exfoliation I ever experienced. Scrapes me down, puts me in some kind of pretzel hold and wrings me out like a dishrag. He brings his face inches from mine and with the thickest of accents he grins, "Turkish culture." I have never been so clean, I walked out into that balmy evening and Istanbul lay before me. How did I get here?

Istanbul, Turkey
Photo: Ruth Wharton

Rock 'n Roll. It was the music that carried me all over the place. The first time I saw a live band play rock and roll, I knew I would be a musician. Four guys with pompadours and matching brocade jackets, all moving together in a sonic dance, making magic. Back when rock and roll was a fledgling genre, I had no idea how revolutionary it would become, but whatever it was, I wanted some. Since I was 15 years old, I've played in bands. I took a break a few times, once to finish college, once to build my cabin in the woods, and I did a solo thing for a few years, but for the rest of my life I played in a band, and most of that time I played my own original music. I'm lucky to have made my living by doing my own thing. But it did not come cheap. Anyone on the blues circuit will tell you it's not easy. Long rides with little sleep, then play, and then ride some more. We once had a month-long tour, playing almost every day, and Virgin Records rearranged our schedule to accommodate a radio show in Paris. This meant that we played a show in Brest, which is on the western tip of Brittany. Then the next day we traveled to Montpellier, on the Mediterranean. So with hardly any sleep, we drove 100 miles per hour all day long, to get there just in time to set up and play. Our drummer sat in the back seat with a towel over his head the entire time shaking with fear. When we arrived at the gig he said, "I quit, I'm goin home." We had some really good Bordeaux and that settled him down enough to finish the tour, but this kind of thing is the half that y'all don't know about. The show is the tip of the iceberg.

Well, after twenty-five years of touring and two heart attacks, I reinvented myself. In 2014, I became a one-man band. Between the new diet, and lightening my workload, I feel the difference. I'm still working my ass off, but it's on my own terms. I simplified my life and eliminated a lot of stress. The high-speed chases, clandestine horticulture, marathon parties and insane touring schedules are now memories. These days I have magical times of playing my music in faraway places, down home or highfalutin, it's ALL good.

Rochester International Jazz Festival
Photo: Ruth Wharton

I've played tiny venues, concert halls, pool parties, blues clubs, schools, listening rooms, city parks, ice cream shops, house parties, nightclubs, restaurants, jukes, homeless shelters and soup kitchens. I've done a Roman Amphitheatre and a Napoleonic Opera House in the south of France and a Laundromat in Tallahassee. Even a bar mitzvah and a nudist colony.

Albert Castiglia, BW, Jimmy Pritchard
Niagara Falls Blues Festival
Photo: Ruth Wharton

Blues en Bourgogne, Le Creusot, France
Photo: Frederic Duverne

County jails and penitentiaries, rib joints, botanical gardens, beaches, pizza parlors, weddings and divorce parties, cruise ships, benefits, art galleries, biker bars and military bases.

Incirlik Airbase. Adana, Turkey
Photo: Ruth Wharton

Funerals and farmers markets. Campgrounds, inaugurations, pubs, and country clubs, bowling alleys, mortgage-burnings, cathedrals, marinas, airports, street corners, and large festivals.

Photo: Ruth Wharton

Thousands of gigs. Over 1,000,000 miles on the highway. Countless flights. Tons of hot sauce. Way over 200,000 people served, and I have never charged a penny for the gumbo. I'm still rolling down the road on an extended vacation with some gigs along the way. A lot of laughter and a lot of tears fell onto these pages. I hope you dug it. But you know what?

Y'all still don't know the half of it.
Chow,
BW

Somewhere Down the Road

Momma told me when I's just a babe
Sang it in that lullaby
Hush little baby don't be afraid
She brushed a tear from my eye
And I can still feel her carrying me
Although she's gone
And I'll never shake that melody
I can still hear the song

Somewhere down the road
I'm gonna drop my heavy load
Put on a brand-new coat
I'm gonna get onboard the boat
Cross the great divide
All the way to the other side
Somewhere down the road

So I'm burning down the highway
My destination unknown
But there's something always carrying me
I have never been alone
I never thought I would get this far
I been taking it on the arm
I got myself a cosmic credit card
Couple o' times, I almost bought the farm

So if I told you I had it down
I'd be telling you a lie
I'm just fun to have around
Gonna make you laugh, make you cry
But there's something always carrying me
To help me with this heavy load
Be that way until they bury me
And I can leave the open road

Thanks, Ruthie Wharton.

Also thanks to: Annie Wharton, Mary Wharton, Floyd Wharton, Kerrie Sandefur, Emma Wharton, Sam Wharton, Rose Wharton, Michael Freedman, Herb Williams, Jerry Duncan, Brian Kirwin, Bill Gwynn, Ed Bell, Jimmy Gear, Joey Hafner, Sally Warner, Tim Goudy, Mark Rutledge, Johnny Brown, Herb Williams, Bob and Sonja Greenlee, Cliff Davis, Jonathan Demme, Chuck Allen, Viviane Signaci, Scott Carswell, Christian di Natale, Louis Adams, Frog, Bob, Don Peyote, Señor Mescalito, Paco, Terra and the Reed Brothers, John Patterson, Mr. Z, Mo and Nancy Davis, Mike Lewis and Fine Resophonic Guitars, Diane Flagler, John Wharton, Sandra Colberg, Susan Massey, Steve Massey, Dick Bangham, Paul Berger, Peach and Dale Hench, J.L. Jamison, Jimmy Buffett, Dave Dewitt, Alan Alovus, Mark Jefferies, Lisa Marie and Terry Geck, Andrew Talbert, J.D. Spradlin, all the citizens of Peckerwood, Jeffrey Clements, James Clements, Raful and Shirley Neal, Peter Mason, Eleanor Crow, Frederic Duverne, Clifford Howes, George Harris, Bob Shacochis, Steve McQueen, Jon Crane, David Kirby, Eric Ilasenko, Jon Nalon, Mickey Adair, Dick Bangham, Kevin Lanigan, Teddy Tollett, Motor City Josh, Glenn Sharron, Scott Sterling, Bobby Shin, David Davidson, Francois Gehin, Mark Rutledge, Randy Scott, and that friend whose name has slipped my mind.

And THANK YOU!!! to all the Musicians: Bill Ande, Mike Andrews, Brian Austin, John Babich, Brian Bassett, Carey Bell, Tab Benoit, Richard Bevis, Bill Blue, Selwyn Birchwood, Mark Blair, Ed Bradley, Ray Brooks, Pat Buchanan, Mick Buchanan, Brian Buck, Albert Castiglia, Tony Coleman, Scott Corwin, Jim Crozier, Barry Cuda, David Davidson, Bo Diddley, Paul Drennan, James Driver, Bruce "Cuz" Durrant, Dennis Everheart, Gary Everling, Jim Farr, Mr.Fisher, Damon Fowler, Velma Frye, Janice Gibbons, Larry Gibson, Bob Greenlee, Jonathan Grooms, Terry Harmon, John Hart, Mike Hart, Justin Headley, Tom Hess, Nick Holmes, Leonard Howell, Steve Howell, Mike Howell, Waldo Hunter, Steve Jacobs, T. A. James, Jim Jarrard, Jim Jenness, Majic John Jones, Mike Jones, Mick Kilgos, Warren "Kingfish" King, Eddie Kirkland, Shannon Kori, Terry Kori, Dick Kraft, David Kuncicky, Pam Laws, Dru Lumbar, Lynne Magin, Michelle Malone, Lisa Mann, Floyd Matthews, Steve Meisburg, Mel Melton, Brian Menendez, David Miller, Chris Miller, Greg Moore, Kenny Neal, John Nemeth, Big Mama Newman, Jerry Newman, Mike Notartomaso, Robert "Freightrain" Parker, Ken Parker, Floyd Pasco, Chris Peet, Pinetop Perkins, John Peterson, Lucky Peterson, Jimmy Pritchard, Pat Ramsey, Tom Rapp, Gary Rasmussen, Rick Redmond, J. R. Richley, Jeff Ridner, Chuck Riley, Pax Robinson, Arthur Rouse, Mitch Sanchez, Donnie Sanchez, Eric Schabacker, Scott Schieve, Tom Schmick, Pat Seery, Erice Shepard, Smaha, Tommy Smith, JP Soars, Mississippi James Stanton, Walter Tates, Jerry Thigpen, Christopher Thomas, Jon Turner, Stan Turner, The Wakulla Band, Louis "Jiggs" Walker, John Walters, Randall "Big Daddy" Webster. Sylvan Wells, David Wharton, Steve Wharton, Mike Wheeler, Sally White, Jassen Wilber, Lon and Lis Williamson. Ron Wilson, Pete Winter, and all the other jammers who jammed the jams.

The Songs

The Recipes

Links

To listen to *The Life and Times of Blind Boy Billy Soundtrack*, here's the audio link: sauceboss.com/bbbsoundtrack

sauceboss.com

planetgumbo.org

The Emperor Wears No Clothes
Content available free at jackherer.com/emperor-3

Forks Over Knives--movie, cookbooks, website, phone app   forksoverknives.com

T. Colin Campbell, *The China Study* nutritionstudies.org

Caldwell B. Esselstyn, Jr., MD, *Prevent and Reverse Heart Disease* dresselstyn.com

John A. McDougall, M.D., *The Starch Solution* www.drmcdougall.com

Dean Ornish, *Reversing Heart Disease* deanornish.com

Rip Esseltyn, *The Engine 2 Diet* engine2diet.com

Happy Herbivore series of cookbooks and blog and meal plans happyherbivore.com

Fat Free Vegan Recipes online fatfreevegan.com

52759702R00077

Made in the USA
Columbia, SC
09 March 2019